YOUR KNOWLEDGE HAS VALUE

- We will publish your bachelor's and master's thesis, essays and papers

- Your own eBook and book - sold worldwide in all relevant shops

- Earn money with each sale

Upload your text at www.GRIN.com and publish for free

Pavel Vasilyev

"Jewish Space" in Fin-De-Siècle Vienna and St. Petersburg: Residential, Occupational and Religious Patterns

GRIN Publishing

Bibliographic information published by the German National Library:

The German National Library lists this publication in the National Bibliography; detailed bibliographic data are available on the Internet at http://dnb.dnb.de .

Imprint:

Copyright © 2010 GRIN Verlag, Open Publishing GmbH
Print and binding: Books on Demand GmbH, Norderstedt Germany
ISBN: 978-3-640-78335-9

This book at GRIN:

http://www.grin.com/en/e-book/163780/jewish-space-in-fin-de-siecle-vienna-and-st-petersburg-residential

GRIN - Your knowledge has value

Since its foundation in 1998, GRIN has specialized in publishing academic texts by students, college teachers and other academics as e-book and printed book. The website www.grin.com is an ideal platform for presenting term papers, final papers, scientific essays, dissertations and specialist books.

Visit us on the internet:

http://www.grin.com/

http://www.facebook.com/grincom

http://www.twitter.com/grin_com

"JEWISH SPACE" IN FIN-DE-SIÈCLE VIENNA AND ST. PETERSBURG: RESIDENTIAL, OCCUPATIONAL AND RELIGIOUS PATTERNS

(Pavel Vasilyev)

At first glance, the historical Jews do not seem to have been a group that was determining the architectural, visual and spatial outlook of cities – in Europe or overseas alike. In fact, as Rudolf Klein put it, "the Jews were seldom in a position – save in ancient and modern Israel – to impose architecture on others"; partially because they "moved so many times in history that they lacked the preconditions for a continuous architectural evolution".[1] Moreover, architecture has always been considered a Jewish 'specialty' much less then, say, literature, medicine or business (at least until recently, as now we have such architecture stars of Jewish descent as Daniel Liebeskind). However, in the pages which follow I will show that a closer look at the connections between the Jews and the urban space is an important and promising enterprise that tells us a lot about the Jews, the city – and also about Gentiles.

The focus of this paper is on the fin-de-siècle period (late 19th – early 20th centuries) and on the two capital cities of Vienna and St. Petersburg – and for some reasons. Both cities were capitals of the empires (Austria-Hungary and the Russian Empire, respectively), that were powerful enough to be a major military and financial competitors, but still technologically and economically backward. The transition to modernity in both capitals was late and problematic, and the Jewish communities have faced a long and persistent anti-Semitism. In both contexts, however, the Jews were especially successful and over-represented in the most modern professions – and also more visible in the rapidly changing modern urban space. Thus, this paper also compliments to the perspective that analyzes "Jewish space" in fin-de-siècle capitals[2] – and brings a comparative element into the picture.

Of course, there are some important limitations to our research that we should recognize. First, residential restrictions in Russia greatly hindered Jewish migration

---

1   Rudolf Klein, "Secession: *un goût juif?* Art Nouveau Buildings and the Jews in some Habsburg Lands," *Jewish Studies at the CEU* 5 (2008): 92, 95.
2   For a study on another empire and its capital, Berlin, see Steven M. Lowenstein, "Jewish Residential Concentration in Post-Emancipation Germany," *Leo Baeck Institute Yearbook* 28 (1983): 471-495.

outside of the Pale of Settlement. This led to the fact that the Viennese Jewish community outnumbered the St. Petersburg one by more than 10 times. Additionally, the nature of political regimes in both countries was different: officially liberal monarchy that emancipated its Jews vs. autocratic and deeply anti-Semitic empire. However, I still believe that the analysis and comparison of "Jewish space" in Vienna and St. Petersburg will be a fruitful enterprise.

Accordingly, in this paper I will look at the Jewish experiences in turn-of-the-century Vienna and St. Petersburg to compare the visions, images and representations of the "Jewish space" in the two imperial capitals that were struggling through modernity. I am particularly interested in residential, occupational and religious aspects of the "Jewish space" as these were the factors that determined the everyday life cycle of particular Jews. Additionally, I want to trace the potential influence that the Jewish patterns of space organization may have exercised upon Gentile ones around turn of the century. In doing so, I plan to rely on such comprehensive volumes that deal with the Jews of fin-de-siècle Vienna and St. Petersburg as (respectively) Marsha L. Rozenblit's "The Jews of Vienna, 1867-1914"[3] and Benjamin Nathans' "Beyond the Pale"[4] – as well as some articles by Rudolf Klein[5], Ivan Davidson Kalmar6 and Ivar Oxaal and Walter R. Weitzmann.[7]

Residential aspect: Jewish homes

We should start our discussion of "Jewish space" in fin-de-siècle Vienna and St. Petersburg with a rather paradoxical cautionary note that there was no one "Jewish space", but rather several areas that could have been recognized as 'Jewish' in one or another way. Neither city had a classical ghetto, which integrated Jewish homes, Jewish businesses, and Jewish synagogues (even though some districts both in Habsburg and Romanov capitals came very close to be named at least quasi-ghettos). As the Jews themselves were not a homogenous group, the differences of class, age and gender

---

3   Marsha L. Rozenblit, *The Jews of Vienna, 1867-1914: Assimilation and Identity* (Albany: State University of New York Press, 1983).
4   Benjamin Nathans, *Beyond the Pale: The Jewish Encounter with Late Imperial Russia* (Berkeley: University of California Press, 2002).
5   Rudolf Klein, "Secession: *un goût juif?* Art Nouveau Building and the Jews in some Habsburg Lands," *Jewish Studies at the CEU* 5 (2008): 91-124.
6   Ivan Davidson Kalmar, "Moorish Style: Orientalism, the Jews, and Synagogue Architecture," *Jewish Social Studies* 7, no. 3 (2001): 68-100.
7   Ivar Oxaal and Walter R. Weitzmann, "The Jews of Pre-1914 Vienna: An Exploration of Basic Sociological Dimensions," *Leo Baeck Institute Yearbook* 30 (1985): 395-432.

greatly influenced the choice of any particular location and its final outlook. In Austrian context, place of origin (Hungary, Galicia, Bohemia, native-born...) was an especially important factor.

The residential habits of the Jews in fin-de-siècle Vienna became a subject of the heated debate between historians of Central Europe. Despite Marsha L. Rozenblit's somewhat simplistic assertion that "the Vienna Jews lived with other Jews"[8], there is a solid evidence of a "wide range of living conditions... from the quasi-ghetto situations of the poorest Galician migrants in the 20th district (Brigittenau) ... to the dispersed, assimilated Jews on the verge of conversion and intermarriage".[9]

The issue of dispersion was actually a major characteristic feature of the Viennese Jewry, especially since the early 20th century. In 1910, about 40% of Viennese Jews "lived across the canal in Leopoldstadt or Brigittenau, the remainder were widely scattered in the city".[10] Diverse Leopoldstadt was in many ways *the* Jewish district *par excellence*. It was "both a reception center for many new immigrants and a permanent habitat for long settled Jewish families".[11] Brigittenau was defined much easier and had mostly pejorative connotations: it was the district of factories, with mostly proletariat population of Czech and Jewish origin; and the local Jews have 'enjoyed' the doubtful reputation of "the most destitute and conspicuous *Ostjuden*".[12]

The other Viennese districts with sizable Jewish communities were of very diverse nature as well: from villa districts of Währing and Döbling to Freud's professional 9th district of Alsergrund (in Rozenblit's words, "*the* neighborhood for Jewish professionals and business employees, the "new" urban Jews"[13]) to industrial Ottakring and proletarian Floridsdorf.[14]

In Russian context, the importance of the Pale experience was still an important factor, which led to the situation when "the territorial dimension was reenacted daily on a smaller scale".[15] There were many voices that daily contributed to the debate about desirability and possibility of Jewish residential segregation (as opposed to ethnic and social intermingling that was almost a must in the metropolitan imperial capital) – both

---

8   Rozenblit, 71.
9   Oxaal and Weitzmann, 405.
10   Ibid., 407.
11   Ibid., 411.
12   Ibid., 411-412.
13   Rozenblit, 89.
14   Oxaal and Weitzmann, 407, 411.
15   Nathans, 113.

on the Jewish and the Gentile sides.

The reality, however, was that the Jews (in absence of any major territorial restrictions within St. Petersburg) actually settled in all twelve of capital's districts (from luxurious Admiralteyskaia to proletarian Vyborgskaia or Rozhdestvenskaia), "but in highly uneven proportions".[16] The most ghetto-like district (nicknamed *Peterburgskii Berdichev*) was formed at the Pod"iacheskie streets, in the center of the city, but still relatively far from the main boulevard of St. Petersburg, Nevsky Avenue.[17]

Perhaps even more important that the actual location, was the inner structure of these Jewish neighborhoods. In Viennese context, as we have already seen, the issue of residential integration/segregation is a subject of debate. Ivar Oxaal and Walter R. Weitzmann state that in the Inner City "a majority of Vienna's early Jewish residents were living in apartment buildings in which they constituted less than fifty percent of the inhabitants".[18] This means that there was a high degree of social intermingling between the Jews and Gentiles (especially for the liberal professions and wealthy capitalists and financiers in the Herrengasseviertel[19]). The situation was radically different on the other side of the Danube canal, in the Leopoldstadt, where "60 percent of the Jewish population lived in buildings where they were to some degree a majority"[20] (especially in the famous building Donau Strasse #4, which at times hosted ca. 5 % (!) of total Viennese Jewish population). Inside the Leopoldstadt, however, there was also a kind of segregation that divided traders and stockmarket personnel living by the canal from petty traders and artisans in the inner sections.[21]

Another perspective is presented by Marsha Rozenblit, who asserts that "Jewishness and not class was the major criterion by which Jews selected a neighborhood".[22] In other words, "Jews lived not in the areas which accorded with their economic status but in Jewish areas"[23] - especially in the Leopoldstadt and Alsergrund. Inside these allegedly 'Jewish' quarters there were separations based on class, wealth

16   Ibid., 117.
17   Ibid., 117-118.
18   Oxaal and Weitzmann, 405-406.
19   Ibid., 406. One of the most important factors that contributed to the intermingling and assimilation, was housing shortage in the Herrengasseviertel and inner Leopoldstadt that led to subletting of apartments (cf. Oxaal and Weitzmann, 406-407).
20   Oxaal and Weitzmann, 406.
21   Ibid.
22   Rozenblit, 94.
23   Ibid., 78.

and also occupational status; rich and poor Jews in the Leopoldstadt would live "in different houses, on different streets, and even on different sections of the ... districts".[24] However, Rozenblit's argument is not absolutely consistent, as she herself gives the examples of class-based choice of residence among Viennese Jews (preference of aristocratic, middle-class, workers' districts to more 'Jewish' ones).[25]

In St. Petersburg context, there seems to be an agreement on an existence of large-scale social intermingling with Gentiles – even in relatively isolated communities of Pod"iacheskie. Interestingly enough, the spatial segregation among St. Petersburg Jews would be based not on the class, occupation or education level, but rather on language. Russian-speaking (probably also more aristocratic) Jews would prefer to live in the center of the city – as opposed to Yiddish-speaking (and also largely working-class) dwellers of the suburbs.[26]

As we can see, the residential habits of the Jews in both Vienna and St. Petersburg were becoming increasingly complex – combining social intermingling with easily recognizable ethnic districts. In a certain way, these more modern forms of residential settlement served as examples not only for the new generations of the Jews arriving in the capitals, but also for the Gentiles.

Occupational aspect: The places to work
One of the most noticeable manifestations of modernity in the urban space is the separation of home and workplace, a process that greatly intensified during the Second Industrial Revolution in Europe[27]. Accordingly, it would be interesting to consider the occupational aspect of the "Jewish space" and compare the Jewish jobs, professions, and businesses in Vienna and St. Petersburg. Our special attention would be drawn to the locations, social structure, and level of income.

In the Habsburg capital, the Jewish workplaces tended to concentrate in two main areas: Inner City and Leopoldstadt. In the center, there were mostly small businesses,[28] and in the Leopoldstadt the majority of the Jews worked as tradesmen of

---

24   Ibid., 83, 85.
25   Ibid., 72-74.
26   Nathans, 120.
27   Rozenblit, 72.
28   Oxaal and Weitzmann, 405.

some sort, doctors or rentiers.[29] In St. Petersburg, the move in the center was slower, and the majority of the Jews tended to work in the traditionally Jewish Pod"iacheskaia districts. This was a voluntary choice to work near the house, as it was encouraged by the infrastructure itself: petty markets, small shops, artisan workshops and brothels all corresponded nicely to the occupational structure of the Jewish population.30

The actual professional stratification of the Jews (especially in the Austrian context) should be addressed by examining a strong association that existed between the Jews and wealth.[31] The work of Ivar Oxaal and Walter R. Weitzmann convincingly shows that the Jews "were not, of course, all rich – indeed very few of them were".[32] Moreover, certain demographic processes that followed the Emancipation in Austria (such as immigration of poor and traditional Jews from Galicia) contributed to the fact that the socio-economic status of the Jews on the whole began to worsen. Indeed, the "ideal types" of the late-nineteenth century Viennese Jewry were not all-mighty bankers and financiers but rather "the peddler, the old-clothes dealer, and the *Lumpenproletarier, scraping an irregular existence on the periphery of the economic system*".[33] Most of the Jews were employed in the trade and transport professions (especially as traders in goods, merchandisers and miscellaneous traders).34 There was also a "rush into clerical and managerial positions"35, but the often assumed re-stratification in the professional sector was in fact very slow.36

In Russian capital, the vast majority of the Jews were registered as merchants, soldiers or *meshchane* (broad social category that included mostly artisans and students).[37] They were involved in the traditional European Jewish occupations as tailors, shoemakers, watchmakers or in the "free professions" as pharmacists, dentists, physicians or lawyers.[38] The often employed possibility to work "at jobs unrelated to …

29   Ibid., 430.
30   Nathans, 117.
31   In another context, a similar association between the Jews and department stores in fin-de-siècle Berlin was nicely deconstructed by Paul Lerner. See Paul F. Lerner, "Circulation and Representation: Jews, Department Stores and Cosmopolitan Consumption in Germany, ca. 1880s-1930s," *European Review of History* 17 (2010) (forthcoming).
32   Oxaal and Weitzmann, 419.
33   Oxaal and Weitzmann, 424 (emphasis added).
34   Ibid., 421-422.
35   Rozenblit, 50.
36   Ibid., 52-53.
37   Nathans, 101. The soldiers were largely the legacy of the 19th century system, and their numbers kept declining, while the percentage of the Jewish *meshchane* population rose consistently.
38   Nathans, 102-103.

official estate status"[39], of course, created additional complications.

Considering the influence that the occupational patterns of the "Jewish space" have exercised upon Gentiles, we should mention that the Jews both in Habsburg lands and in Russia (though to a lesser degree in the latter) were at the forefront of modernity. As such, they were the role models, and their earlier entrance into bureaucracy and professions served as an example for the generations of Gentiles that followed.

Religious patterns: The places of Jewish worship
The synagogue is the center of Jewish religious life, one of the major components of Jewish identity and arguably the most visible manifestation of Jewishness in the urban space. It is not surprisingly then, that we should also consider the location and the outlook of major synagogues in the two imperial capitals.

In Vienna, there was a classical Biedermaier style central synagogue hided among the facades of Seitenstettengasse in the Inner City (built in 1826).[40] However, the largest synagogue, Leopoldstädter Tempel, was erected in Leopoldstadt from 1853-1858 by Ludwig Förster – and it was built in a recognizably Moorish style. Among other notable synagogues were "the Polish synagogue" of Wilhelm Stiassny (1892-1893) and the Art Nouveau building in Döbling (1907).

In St. Petersburg, the choice of the place for the Grand Choral Synagogue (built 1880-1888) was a very complicated process as the topic itself had not only religious but also political connotations. The first attempts were made in 1869, but the negotiations lasted for about ten years.[41] Finally, the place was chosen on Bolshaia Masterskaia Street (now Lermontovskii Avenue), close to the Mariinskii Opera House (but still in a somewhat provincial district of minor officials and artisans - not far away from the Pod"iacheskie settlements).

Interestingly enough, the architecture of the major synagogues in both Vienna and St. Petersburg shared many important characteristics. The Leopoldstädter Tempel was in many ways the epitome of the mid-19th century Moorish style. Flirting with Islamic motives in the construction of synagogues - ornamental towers, large

---

39   Ibid., 107.
40   Oxaal and Weitzmann, 405.
41   Nathans, 159-164.

medallions on the facade etc.[42] - was the sign of Otherness *par excellence*. For the Jews, these were Orientalist idealizations, "expression of ... quest" to "convince the public of the nobility of their Oriental blood"[43] and connection with the ancient tradition - particularly the Solomon's Temple.[44] For the Gentiles, however, Orientalism was often a shortcut to clearly distinguish the Jews, as outsiders, "Asiates of Europe".[45]

In Russian capital, the synagogue built with the pretentious premise that it "must not be inferior in any way to the synagogues of other countries and capitals"[46] was also encapsulated in the Moorish form – but not without previous discussion. At the first glance, it would seem only logical that the most westernized Russian Jewish community[47] would follow the mainstream European trends and adopt the Oriental style. There were, however, acute discussions, and the alternatives proposed included the imitation of Russian Orthodox style (as throughout their history the Jews tended to borrow the styles of the dominant nations) or avoidance of Moorish style as too associated with the alleged 'Protestantism' of Berlin Oranienburger Strasse synagogue.[48] The final result, however, was such an unmistakably recognizable Eastern product with pseudo-minarets and many ornamental details that Osip Mandel'shtam even called it "an exotic fig tree".[49]

Synagogue architecture also provides us a nice angle to look at the connections between the Jews, "Jewish space" and the broader public. In fact, some authors have claimed that not only did the Jews provide financial and intellectual support for the *Sezession* movement, but the whole project of fin-de-siècle architecture can be described as 'Jewish' (in a sense close to the word 'modern').[50]

In conclusion, I would like to summarize some major findings of the paper. As we have seen, there is a previously unnoticed and probably unexpected degree of similarity between the two capitals. Of course, the "Jewish space" in Vienna was in

42   Kalmar, 79, 83-84.
43   Ibid., 72.
44   Ibid., 78-79.
45   Klein, 105.
46   Nathans, 155-156.
47   Kalmar, 85.
48   Nathans, 157-158.
49   Ibid., 164.
50   Klein, 99-102, and *passim*. Cf. also Yuri Slezkine, *The Jewish Century* (Princeton: Princeton University Press, 2004).

some ways more modern than in St. Petersburg. Undoubtedly, the explanation of this fact would be linked to the political, cultural and technological backwardness of the Russian Empire. However, in both contexts the changes in residential, occupational and religious patterns of the "Jewish space" actually reflected the ongoing processes of modernization that the communities in both capitals were dealing with. It is also strikingly clear, that some of the trends that were born in the "Jewish space" were later successfully transplanted to the Gentile soil. In fact, the arrival of modernity not only brought the amelioration of Jewish legal standing, but also the hope of transforming the whole world into the Holy Land[51] - and the urban landscape was the very space to begin this transformation.

Perspectives for further research may include involvement of other national contexts, which provide possibility to compare data regarding residential, occupational and religious strategies of the Jews for the same period of time (even though, a certain portion of the data may be unreliable or incomparable due to the differences in size, origin and socio-economic status of the Jewish populations in different countries). Other potentially interesting directions would lead us to a closer analysis of primary sources, especially ego documents and the press.

---

51   Klein, 98.

Bibliography

1.   Kalmar, Ivan Davidson. "Moorish Style: Orientalism, the Jews, and Synagogue Architecture." *Jewish Social Studies* 7, no. 3 (2001): 68-100.

2.   Klein, Rudolf. "Secession: *un goût juif?* Art Nouveau Buildings and the Jews in some Habsburg Lands." *Jewish Studies at the CEU* 5 (2008): 91-124.

3.   Lerner, Paul F. "Circulation and Representation: Jews, Department Stores and Cosmopolitan Consumption in Germany, ca. 1880s-1930s." *European Review of History* 17 (2010) (forthcoming)

4.   Lowenstein, Steven M. "Jewish Residential Concentration in Post-Emancipation Germany." *Leo Baeck Institute Yearbook* 28 (1983): 471-495.

5.   Nathans, Benjamin. *Beyond the Pale: The Jewish Encounter with Late Imperial Russia.* Berkeley: University of California Press, 2002.

6.   Oxaal, Ivar and Walter R. Weitzmann. "The Jews of Pre-1914 Vienna: An Exploration of Basic Sociological Dimensions." *Leo Baeck Institute Yearbook* 30 (1985): 395-432.

7.   Rozenblit, Marsha L. *The Jews of Vienna, 1867-1914: Assimilation and Identity.* Albany: State University of New York Press, 1983.

8.   Slezkine, Yuri. *The Jewish Century.* Princeton: Princeton University Press, 2004.